MASS
APPEAL

BY BILL C. DAVIS

★ Revised Edition

★

DRAMATISTS
PLAY SERVICE
INC.

MASS APPEAL was first presented by the Manhattan Theatre Club in New York City on May 11, 1980. It was directed by Geraldine Fitzgerald; the set design was by David Gropman; the costume design was by William Ivey Long; and the lighting design was by F. Mitchell Dana. The cast was as follows:

FATHER TIM FARLEY ....…… Milo O'Shea
MARK DOLSON ....… Eric Roberts

The Manhattan Theatre Club production of MASS APPEAL was subsequently presented by Elizabeth I. McCann, Nelle Nugent and Ray Larsen, in association with Lynne Meadow, Barry Grove, and Warner Theatre Productions, Inc. on Broadway at the Booth Theatre on November 12, 1981. The director was Geraldine Fitzgerald; the set design was by David Gropman; the costume design was by William Ivey Long; and the lighting design was by F. Mitchell Dana. The cast was as follows:

FATHER TIM FARLEY ....… Milo O'Shea
MARK DOLSON ....…… Michael O'Keefe

CHARACTERS

FATHER TIM FARLEY

MARK DOLSON

PLACE

The action of the play takes place in
Father Tim Farley's office and in St. Francis Church.

TIME

It is autumn.

SCENE BREAKDOWN

ACT ONE

Scene 1: Sunday morning, 10:15 mass
Scene 2: Wednesday afternoon
Scene 3: Friday, one week later
Scene 4: Sunday, one week later, 10:15 mass
Scene 5: That afternoon

ACT TWO

Scene 1: Immediately after the 5:20 mass
Scene 2: Sunday, next week, 5:20 mass
Scene 3: Monday morning
Scene 4: 10:15 mass, that Sunday
Scene 5: That afternoon
Scene 6: 5:20 mass

MASS APPEAL

ACT ONE

Scene 1

Sunday morning. Tim is in the pulpit.

TIM. In the name of the Father and of the Son and of the Holy Spirit, Amen. Today we are concluding our 3-C series. For newcomers here to St. Francis, that's "Current Crises in Catholicism." Our next series will be the most important and inspiring I've ever given. I don't know what it is yet, but it will begin next Sunday — so don't miss it. Last night, while I was thinking about our 3-C series, I fell asleep — straining over the most recent crisis facing our church today. Consequently, I dreamt that (Hillary Clinton/Tipper Gore/Janet Reno/Rosie O'Donnell) was ordained a priest. You guessed it — the question we have to ask ourselves this morning is: Should women be priests? I remember when the *big* moral question of the day was, "Should we chew the host or let it melt in our mouths?" I think that today's crisis is controversial enough to open it up to a dialogue sermon. Now I'm sure you've all done some thinking about this subject, and we've had dialogue sermons before. They can be lots of fun if we're not shy, so let's … *(Points L.)* Yes — Mrs. Curry. *(He listens.)* Well — the reason the Pope gives is that priests should be in the image of Christ. Now that's what *he* says but he is not speaking "ex cathedra." In other words, that decision is not infallible. So there's hope for you yet, Mrs. Curry. *(Points.)* Yes — Mrs. Hart. *(He listens.)* No — Being in the image of Christ does not mean I'll have to grow a beard, Mrs. Hart. And even if I had to, I wouldn't. A beard would make me look at least ten years older. *(Points.)* Yes — in the back. *(Mark Dolson's voice is heard from the rear of the church.)*

MARK. What do *you* think of women becoming priests?

TIM. What do *I* think? Well ... I don't like to sway people's viewpoints so I'll plead the Fifth on that one.

MARK. *(Coming down the aisle.)* Yes — but this is a dialogue sermon.

TIM. I know it's a dialogue sermon.

MARK. And dialogue means ...

TIM. I know what dialogue means. Is this your first visit to our church? *(Lights come up where he is standing. He is wearing grey sweat pants, a red sweat-jacket and sneakers.)*

MARK. Yes.

TIM. Well — welcome. *(Points.)* Yes — Mr. Quinn.

MARK. I haven't given my unswayed viewpoint yet.

TIM. That's true — you haven't.

MARK. I think women should be priests.

TIM. You look rather familiar. Where are you from?

MARK. I attend St. Francis Seminary.

TIM. That's where I've seen you before. Give your rector, Monsignor Burke, my best regards when you see him. *(Turns away from Mark.)* Now — Mr. Quinn.

MARK. Don't you want to know *why* I think women should be priests?

TIM. *(Pause. Motions helplessly to Mr. Quinn.)* By all means — Don't be shy.

MARK. Well — you said that priests should be in the image of Christ.

TIM. No, I did not say that. The Pope did.

MARK. Whoever. But when Christ was crucified, only three people stayed with him to the very end and two of the three were women. At the foot of this cross was his youngest apostle ...

TIM. St. John ...

MARK. ...his mother ...

TIM. *(Concurring.)* right ... his mother ...

MARK. And an ex-hooker. *(Pause — Tim is taken aback.)* All of the men either denied him or were hiding out. On the way to being crucified — it was a woman who pushed through a hostile crowd and wiped all the blood and "male" spit off his face. The first person he appeared to after his resurrection was Mary Magdalene. I really feel that the courage and loyalty these women showed the actual person Jesus *is* in his image, and I think it's foolish to continue depriving ourselves of the beautiful qualities a woman could bring to the priesthood.

TIM. You really should invest in a portable pulpit. Now — Mr. Quinn. *(Silence.)* You forgot what you were going to say? Well — *(Looks to Mark, then back.)* That happens. Anyone else? *(Silence.)* No one? *(Pause.)* Oh, come on — I saw some hands up before ... *(Silence.)* Aaaaaalright. I have two announcements this morning *(Reading from a sheet of paper.)* First, there's bingo Tuesday evening at eight o'clock in Mother Cabrini Hall — or Cabrini's casino as I prefer to call it. And will the owner of a blue Lexus license number DU-324 — please move it — you're blocking the exit. I strongly advise whoever you are to move the car as quickly as possible because after mass a church exit is the most dangerous passage in the world. Let us pray. *(Lights go to black.)*

Scene 2

Lights immediately come up on the office. Wednesday afternoon. Mark is there in his running clothes. Tim enters.

TIM. So — Mark Dolson.
MARK. *(Shakes hands with Tim.)* Father Farley —
TIM. I only have a few minutes but this won't take long. *(Noticing Mark's sweat suit.)* Is this the seminarian's new uniform?
MARK. I wasn't sure I should come dressed this way, but ...
TIM. *(Looking at Mark's sneakers.)* I hope you didn't track mud across Margaret's nice clean floors.
MARK. *(Looking to see if there is mud on bottom of sneakers.)* Sorry.
TIM. Was it necessary that you run here?

9

MARK. I try to keep a schedule — eight miles a day. It's four miles between here and the seminary so I'll run the other four when I leave.

TIM. I'm glad you could fit me in.

MARK. It's just that I always do the eight miles around this time. When you called, I said "yes" to this time without thinking.

TIM. There's actually a time when you're *not* thinking?

MARK. *(Pause.)* Sometimes, I think more clearly than at other times. When I'm on the phone I don't think very clearly.

TIM. You think very clearly at mass.

MARK. I feel at home in church.

TIM. That was very apparent last Sunday. *(Pause.)* Tell me — why do you think women are better than men?

MARK. I didn't say they were better. They're more loyal.

TIM. What makes you say that?

MARK. *(Pause.)* Is this why you wanted to see me?

TIM. Do you know that I am an advisor at your seminary?

MARK. Yes — *(Tim gets a wine bottle and two glasses.)* Father DeNicola plays tapes of your sermons in our homily class and the faculty talk about you a lot. They seem very proud that you're on their "team." But I never see you there.

TIM. The parish keeps me very busy. *(Starts pouring wine into glasses.)* Anyway — I asked some of the faculty about you and from my description of you they knew you instantly. And from what they say, you have quite a reputation.

MARK. Really?

TIM. And you certainly lived up to that reputation last Sunday.

MARK. Did I?

TIM. Yes — and so I wanted to tell you how much I admired the things you were saying during my mass, and don't ever do anything like that again. *(Offers glass to Mark.)*

MARK. *(Refuses wine with hand gesture.)* Why not?

TIM. You were challenging me in front of my congregation. I don't like that.

MARK. I took a stand.

TIM. No, you did not take a stand. You took a *grand*stand. Besides — you're a seminarian — and if you want to become a deacon, you should be going to mass at the seminary.

MARK. Believe me — I prefer to go to mass at the seminary.

TIM. Then why didn't you?

MARK. Because the rector sent me to yours.

TIM. Monsignor Burke?

MARK. Yes.

TIM. Monsignor Burke sent you to my mass?

MARK. Yes.

TIM. Did he say why he was sending you?

MARK. He said that you were the most tactful priest in the diocese, and that tact was something I needed to learn.

TIM. *(Laughs.)* He really is something.

MARK. You're not the most tactful priest in the diocese?

TIM. I might be — but that's not why he sent you.

MARK. It's not?

TIM. No.

MARK. Well — why do *you* think he sent me?

TIM. Because he wanted to get back at me for canceling a dinner engagement with him.

MARK. I'm sorry — I don't understand.

TIM. He gets very upset when I cancel anything with him, but he never shows it. So he does something more subtle. For example, he knows your reputation — he knows my dialogue sermons, so he put the two together hoping for exactly what happened. In other words, you did what he wanted you to do.

MARK. If I was used as a pawn, that's the players' problem, not mine.

TIM. If you want to be a priest in the same church as the players, it is your problem.

MARK. *(Pause.)* Do you cancel dinner with him often?

TIM. Is that any of your business?

MARK. You just said — it is my problem. I should get to know the church hierarchy — monsignors, advisors — why did you cancel?

TIM. Someone in the parish had a problem and I couldn't get away.

MARK. Really?

TIM. You don't believe that?

MARK. No.

TIM. Very good. You shouldn't. Actually he and his sister had pictures of a trip the three of us took to Barcelona. And they wanted to get together with me over dinner to look at the pictures.

MARK. Why didn't you?

TIM. The only thing I can imagine worse than the trip itself would be pictures of the trip. *(Silence.)* It was a harmless lie.

MARK. I didn't know there was such a thing.

TIM. Well — worse that that — it was a useless lie. *(Tim laughs — Mark doesn't.)*

MARK. Can I go now? It's not good to break up the eight miles this much.

TIM. Certainly … *(Mark starts to leave.)* If you'd rather skip the rest of your run, I can give you a lift. *(Mark turns.)* I have to go to the seminary anyway. I have a meeting with Monsignor Burke. About two seminarians. Wait a minute. *(He takes a page from a note pad on the desk.)* Maybe you might know something. *(Reading.)* "Frank Kearney and Alfred Varasi." — do you know them?

MARK. Yeah — fairly well. They work with the emotionally disturbed children every Tuesday and Thursday. I watch them — they're good.

TIM. It seems they're together a lot.

MARK. They're best friends.

TIM. How do you know?

MARK. I usually see them together during the day, so I assume …

TIM. I probably shouldn't be discussing this with you, but this meeting was prompted by rumors which have been reaching Monsignor Burke that not only are they together all day, but all night as well. Do you know if that's true?

MARK. No — I don't. But so what if they are?

TIM. Don't play innocent, Mark. When I was at the seminary we could only travel in threes. Things have loosened up a little since then. But there are still strong taboos. Frank and Alfred are fooling around with the ultimate tabu.

MARK. They haven't taken any vows yet.

TIM. There's serious question they'll be allowed to — ever.

MARK. That's ridiculous — one meeting can't decide that.

TIM. You're right. These meetings never decide anything. They only help Monsignor Burke decide.

MARK. How are you going to advise him?

TIM. The only purpose of the rector's advisor is to find out exactly what the rector really wants to do and then advise him to do that.

MARK. That must make you feel awfully insignificant.

TIM. Yes — well — I'd love to discuss this with you further, but if I don't leave now, I'll be late. And the one thing he loves more than chastity is punctuality. *(Mark starts to leave.)* Are you sure I can't give you a lift?

MARK. *(Stops and turns.)* Is that your Mercedes out front?

TIM. Yes.

MARK. I'd rather run. *(Pause.)* Listen — I don't know if yours and Monsignor Burke's game rules apply to seminarians, but I hope you won't use your position at the seminary over me. I only spoke up at your mass because it was important to me. Becoming a priest is important to me. *(He comes closer to Tim.)* Please don't play games with it. *(The lights black out as Mark starts to exit. Tim is still. During the blackout, we hear a recording of Tim's voice.)*

Scene 3

The office.

Friday. One week later.

TIM'S VOICE. *(His taped sermon is heard in the darkness.)* Last week — the rector, Monsignor Burke, and I and the faculty of St. Francis Seminary met to decide which seminarians should become deacons. So what better time to begin our ... *(The lights come up on Tim.)* "On the Road to the Priesthood Series" ... Being a deacon is the last step before becoming a priest. A deacon must take a vow of celibacy. He can then preach, give out communion, visit the sick, teach religion and counsel. *(He goes to the tape recorder.)* Being a deacon is primarily and most importantly a big pain in the ass. *(He stops the tape recorder. Rewinds. Stops it again. Presses record.)* Neck. *(To himself.)* Hold for laugh. There is a rumor going around the parish that I was *born* a priest. *(To himself.)* Hold for laugh. This is not true. It was a long journey from the seminary, to this pulpit here at St. Francis. The most horrible part of the journey, for me, was being a deacon. Every Sunday, for an entire summer, as part of my training, I had to give sermons from a soap box on a street corner. Can you picture that? *(Refers to his notes.)* For the first month it seemed as if the only people who stopped to listen were four tall men dressed in gray suits. I was convinced that these four men were FBI agents trying to figure out which one of the Berrigan brothers I might be. For those of you in the congregation who are too young to know who the Berrigans are, they are two brave priests who always got in trouble for what they believed were the right reasons, and to whom I bear no resemblance. But the four tall men in gray suits were not taking any chances. There they were, every Sunday, in the middle of the blazing sun, waiting for me to say something dangerous. *(To himself.)* Hold for laugh — maybe. *(Pause.)* But other people did stop. Shoppers, students, workers on their lunch hours — all kinds of people. And we ... talked. Isn't it funny? I don't remember so much what they said — as much as I remember what they wore. They were just regular, everyday people. Women in light-colored dresses — young men in shorts — old men in faded plaid shirts — just about everyone wore some kind of sandal, and I know I haven't been as close to Christ — since. *(Tim stops not sure what he's just said. He stops the tape, then rewinds. After he presses a button to play back, we hear:)*

TIM'S VOICE. Old men in faded plaid shirts — just about everyone wore some kind of sandal, and I know I haven't been as close to Christ — since. *(House phone buzzes. Tim answers.)* Yes, Margaret ... Good. Send him in. *(He hangs up. Mark enters but stays close to entrance. Tim, seeing Mark.)* Come in.

MARK. *(Not moving.)* Hello, Father.

TIM. I see you're still in uniform.

MARK. Did you want to see me about something important?

TIM. Tell me — do you do a lot of exercising besides the running?

MARK. Yes.

TIM. Working out your hostilities?

MARK. No — I don't have any hostilities; I'm preparing for celibacy.

TIM. Well, you may not have to.

MARK. *(Coming into the room.)* What did you say?

TIM. You may not have to prepare for celibacy — or the priesthood.

MARK. *(Going to Tim.)* What are you talking about?

TIM. Monsignor Burke has been having second thoughts about several seminarians. During our last meeting — your name came up.

MARK. Why?

TIM. He said that you were immature, and he felt very strongly that you weren't ready to become a deacon.

MARK. He has no reason to say that.

TIM. He suggested you take off a year from your studies to decide whether or not you really want to be a priest, which, as you'll learn, is Latin for "Get lost."

MARK. I'll kill him.

TIM. But without hostility, of course.

MARK. *(Starts to leave.)* I'm going to talk to him.

TIM. Mark — wait.

MARK. Am I being used as a pawn again?

TIM. No.

MARK. Then why are you telling me all this? Why isn't Monsignor Burke?

TIM. I'll explain, if you'll slow down.

MARK. I thought everything was decided.

TIM. It was.

MARK. What happened?

TIM. Don't you know?

MARK. No — I don't.

TIM. I spoke to Monsignor Burke after the meeting, and he told me that last Wednesday, you stormed into his office and attacked him on his decision to force a leave of absence on Frank Kearney and Alfred Virasi.

MARK. I did not attack. I expressed my opinion.

TIM. And in the course of expressing your opinion, did you call him a "homophobic autocrat?"

MARK. Yes.

TIM. Mark ... if you want to become a priest, you can't do things like that.

MARK. I had to.

TIM. Why do you feel you have to be the knight errant?

MARK. Look ... you're never at the seminary. You don't see it. Nobody there cares what going on. Do you know how many seminarians have TVs in their rooms? Most of their praying and meditating is done during commercials. They all drive brand new freshly simonized cars. They take off for St. Thomas and California like I go to the movies. But that's fine with Monsignor Burke. Somehow *that* fits in with his definition of ecumenism. But he hears a few rumors about Frank and Alfred and he gets out his trumpet to blow down the walls of Sodom and Gomorrah.

TIM. Mark — save it. I spoke to Monsignor Burke on your behalf, and you're going to be made a deacon next Wednesday, just like the rest of them. But from what I can see — and hear, you're not like the rest of them.

MARK. *(Pause.)* Thank you for your help with Monsignor Burke.

TIM. That's all right.

MARK. Is there anything else?

TIM. As a matter of fact — there is. My good deed did not go unpunished. You have been assigned to me.

MARK. What?

TIM. You've been assigned to me. Monsignor Burke let you by with reservation and on condition that I work with you.

MARK. *(Stands.)* I don't want to be a special assignment.

TIM. Fine — then you'll never be a deacon and I'll have less work to do.

MARK. What does he think you'll teach me that I won't be taught at the seminary?

TIM. Contrary to what you may think I am considered to be one of the best priests in this diocese. I'm not bragging — that's just how things are.

MARK. You're popular — that doesn't mean you can teach me what I need to learn.

TIM. You — don't want to be popular?

MARK. No.

TIM. Do you want to be a priest?

MARK. Yes.

TIM. Then shut up and do what I tell you. *(Mark sits.)* Now before we begin — as a rule — is this day good for you? Friday?

MARK. No.

TIM. Oh. Well, what about Thursday?

MARK. No good either.

TIM. Why not?

MARK. The senior citizen center has a dance every Thursday afternoon and I play the piano for them.

TIM. I see. Well, what about Wednesday?

MARK. No.

TIM. What happens Wednesday?

MARK. CTA meeting.

TIM. CTA?

MARK. Call To Action.

TIM. What, I am terrified to ask, is Call To Action?

MARK. It's a Catholic group that believes the Church has an obligation to initiate programs of peace and justice in the world. You've never heard of it?

TIM. Please, I'm a simple parish priest. All right — so you'll be initiating programs of peace and justice on Wednesday. How about Tuesday?

MARK. Prison.

TIM. So Tuesday's no good either. Well, Monday is no good for me. I go to the races. I go to the races on Monday to get over the masses on Sunday. So that leaves today. Now tell me I'm keeping you from a leper colony. Let's just decide every Friday so we can get to work. *(Pushes phone button for Margaret.)* Margaret, listen — I have one appointment this afternoon which I will have to cancel … never mind why. Mr. & Mrs. Koyn — *(To Mark.)* They're worried. They've been married for twenty-three years; they've never had a fight. *(Back to phone.)* Margaret — listen, I made the appointment with Mrs. Koyn so tell Mr. Koyn she mixed up the date. *(To Mark.)* See what that gets started … It's not a lie, Margaret. It's creative counseling … Now, Margaret — we've talked about your scruples before … All right, all right — just tell the Koyns to call me next week. Thank you Margaret. *(He hangs up.)* The word scruples comes from the Latin meaning pebbles. Margaret is a veritable boulder. *(Picks up folders from the desk.)* Now I've had long talks with the faculty and I've met with Monsignor Burke — over dinner, you'll be happy to hear. And from these meetings I've broken down our work into three lessons.

MARK. "Lessons" — what is this? Remedial reading?

TIM. No. It's structure.

MARK. I'm all for structure — but "lessons"?

TIM. You can call them what you like — I'm calling them lessons. *(Tim takes out a bottle of sparkling Burgundy. Tim sees Mark staring at it.)* A gift from the congregation, *(Tim goes to desk.)* Lesson I — Sermons. *(Tim pours himself a glass of wine and opens sermon folder.)* At some point, you'll be expected to give a sermon. Father DeNicola gave me some of your sermons from his class, which I haven't had a chance to look at yet. Let's take your most recent one and go over that together. *(Tim pulls it out of folder.)*

TIM. Do you have it memorized?

MARK. Yes — but you have it right here. Can't you just read it?

TIM. *(Picks up sermon and red pencil.)* No. I want to hear your technique.

MARK. My technique?

TIM. Yes. I've seen what you can do when someone else is in the pulpit, but it's different when you're in there yourself.

MARK. *(Positioning himself.)* Jesus is not impressed with your Gap shirts, your cell phones and your blue hair."

TIM. Never say "you" or "your." It's "we" and "our" — always. *(Pencils in changes.)*

MARK. What are you doing?

TIM. Making the correction. Go on.

MARK. "Jesus is not impressed with *our* Gap shirts and our cell phones and ... our blue hair"?

TIM. Cut the "blue hair." Go on.

MARK. "Those things are our shackles. They dim our vision. They ... " What's the rest?

TIM. Skip it. If you can't remember a part of a sentence, it usually doesn't belong. Go on.

MARK. How far can we go? How long before light and air can't penetrate the clutter of objects with which *we* shower ourselves?

TIM. Scratch the "with which." Just say "Which we shower ourselves with."

MARK. Sermons can't be grammatically correct?

TIM. Sermons should be understood. Proper grammar doesn't

18

necessarily help understanding.

MARK. And I don't shower myself with objects.

TIM. Your family does.

MARK. How do you know that?

TIM. Monsignor Burke showed me your family's official Christmas card: A magnificent fireplace — Chippendale furniture — and a smiling English setter picturesquely posed before a roaring hearth.

MARK. Maybe my family does shower themselves with objects, but I don't. And I don't wear Gap shirts, why do I have to say "we?"

TIM. I'm only telling you what works.

MARK. And if "what works" isn't the truth ... ?

TIM. Mark — do you like my sermons?

MARK. Well ... No.

TIM. What do you mean, "Well ... no?" I have to sign autographs after every mass.

MARK. I never liked song and dance theology.

TIM. I see. Monsignor Burke is a homophobic autocrat and I'm Father Bojangles.

MARK. Maybe things were different when *you* were growing up, but when I was a teenager, the church was a circus. Everyone sang Top 40 tunes at mass. Didn't matter if they related. I remember once, on Ascension Thursday — the day Jesus ultimately transcends this world, and body and soul enters Heaven, the hip hymn committee sang, "Leavin' on a Jet Plane." When I was in the second grade, my religion teacher's Bible was the "Gospel According to Peanuts." So I spent a year thinking Jesus was a beagle. Let me say what I want from the pulpit. I think people will respect that. They feel more secure with someone who states his position clearly.

TIM. *(Pours more wine into glass.)* State it as clearly as you like. If it's not their position, they'll turn on you.

MARK. Then the only reason you give sermons is to be liked?

TIM. I like being liked. It gives me a warm feeling. That and wine are the only warmth I get. I'm not about to give up either. *(Takes a drink.)*

MARK. You'll be liked much more for being real and sober.

TIM. Well — this is a great way to begin. So far, you have called me a song and a dance theologian, a phony and a drunkard. I am your teacher.

19

MARK. I respect standards — not positions.

TIM. You don't have to respect my position or me. But the one thing I insist you respect is my congregation. You'll be giving a sermon during my mass, and I'll tell you straight off — you're not giving this "kick-ass" sermon to my congregation.

MARK. A congregation that keeps you well stocked in sparkling Burgundy. And why do you drink so much?

TIM. I have never missed a mass, a class or an appointment in my entire career as a priest. Never.

MARK. You just cancelled one …

TIM. Cancelling is not missing. And I'll have you know further, that during this past week alone, this drunken minstrel has met *and* dealt with four broken marriages … ten identity crises … three potential abortions and seven "I don't know why I'm alives."

MARK. And I bet you were too easy on all of them. That's how you are from the pulpit.

TIM. The pulpit is not the place to ventilate.

MARK. I know — but there *are* serious social and moral conditions that can be tended to from the pulpit.

TIM. Mark — your sermon sucks.

MARK. You haven't heard the rest.

TIM. The rest could be the Sermon on the Mount. *(Picks up sermon.)* But after two minutes of this they'd just turn you off.

MARK. I can't believe that.

TIM. It's not a question of faith. It's the cold hard facts of the pulpit.

MARK. What are you suggesting I do?

TIM. I'm not suggesting — I'm telling you — don't kick ass.

MARK. Better that than to kiss it.

TIM. *(Tim stares at Mark. He tears up the sermon. Mark starts to leave.)* Mark — *(Mark stops.)* Mark, I'm doing this for your own good. Monsignor Burke can keep you as a deacon for the next ten years. The only thing that can influence Monsignor Burke more than I can is the congregation. So I want you to give a friendly sermon. Every sermon has a theme. There are "what if" sermons; there are "remember when" sermons, and there are "why" sermons. "Why" sermons are the most fundamental. So we'll start you off on a "why" sermon. Your theme will be "why go to mass?"

MARK. "Why go to mass?"

TIM. "Why go to mass" … And don't be afraid to be charming. There's nothing wrong with being charming. Be personal. Talk about yourself. For example — Did you and your family go to mass together?

MARK. Yes — but …

TIM. Did you wear a suit?

MARK. What difference would that make?

TIM. They need to see you in a nice Norman Rockwell setting. Did you wear a suit?

MARK. Yes. No. Well, it was more like an outfit, really.

TIM. An outfit?

MARK. Yeah — you know.

TIM. No — I don't.

MARK. Well — I had a red sports coat — with gold buttons — they looked like Roman coins. And a vest — houndstooth check — and a clip-on tie because I couldn't tie a regular tie.

TIM. I see *(Looking for another angle.)* Were you good in church?

MARK. No.

TIM. Even then. What would you do that was so bad?

MARK. I'd laugh a lot.

TIM. Why?

MARK. Well — you know — something would strike me as funny and I'd laugh. Someone's stomach would rumble in the middle of the consecration — or a baby would throw his mother's hat in the aisle — and I'd laugh — and knowing I wasn't supposed to laugh made it hard to stop — and trying to stop just sent me into hysterics. A few times my father had to pull me outside.

TIM. Did he hit you?

MARK. No — He never hit me.

TIM. That's good.

MARK. He shook me a few times. Why did you ask that? Is that part of the Norman Rockwell setting?

TIM. No. None of this is, really. What about after mass? Where would you and your family go after mass?

MARK. The bakery.

TIM. Really? Now that's more like it. That's nice. What would you get?

MARK. Jelly doughnuts.

TIM. That is great! Now that just the kind of thing you have to go for.

MARK. People don't go to mass to hear about bakeries.

TIM. Mark — I've been at this for awhile and that's exactly what they want to hear. And that's what they're going to hear the first Sunday there's an opening in our calendar of Sunday events. So I want you to be ready immediately.

MARK. Immediately?

TIM. Yes — cancellations can come at any time. *(Tim ushers Mark out.)* I want you to go back to the seminary and start work on your jelly doughnut sermon. Wait! Come back! *(Mark comes back to Tim.)* This is very important — You must always have an alternate sermon ready in case the one you're giving isn't working.

MARK. How will I know if the sermon I'm giving isn't working?

TIM. Coughs.

MARK. Coughs?

TIM. Coughs. If you hear a lot of coughs that means they're bored. And if they start dropping their missals, that's trouble too.

MARK. This is ridiculous. How can the spirit move me if I'm listening for coughs and people dropping books?

TIM. The "spirit" move you? ... Mark — here are the facts of this particular campaign we're about to embark on. If the people in my parish think you're cute and witty, this opinion will find its way back to the seminary and Monsignor Burke, who will immediately begin proceedings for your canonization. But if the people in my parish think you are what they used to call at the seminary a "Bangladesh Granola Head," this too will find its way back to the seminary and you'll be immediately shipped off to a Trappist Monastery in the mountains and put to work in a rustic bakery. Now those are your choices.

MARK. What do they bake there? *(Blackout.)*

Scene 4

The church.

Sunday morning — Tim addresses the congregation.

TIM. Today — we were supposed to see Sister Rosalie and her Maryknoll Marionettes. But unfortunately sister Claire accidentally slammed the car door on Sister Rosalie's hand. Nothing serious — but she operates the bottom part of the puppet with that hand, so we'll have to wait. As I look around this morning I see we have some of the members of the faculty from St. Francis Seminary with us. And I have a treat for all of us. In keeping with our "On the Road to the Priesthood Series," we are going to hear a first sermon. This is a young man who was just installed as a deacon last Wednesday. Some of you may remember him from our last dialogue sermon. There's a certain James Dean quality about him that I think you'll find very exciting. Would you welcome please — Deacon Dolson. *(Tim leaves the pulpit, Mark enters wearing his white alb. He goes into the pulpit and turns to Tim.)*
MARK. Thank you, Father Farley. *(Tim exits. Mark faces the congregation.)* It's funny — I never stopped to think that on my way to becoming a priest I'd have to live with the name, Deacon Dolson. It sounds pretty silly, don't you think? "Deacon Dolson." *(A single cough — He freezes.)* Can I ask all of us a question? Why did we come to mass today? What brought us to church this morning? As a teenager I had a friend who answered this question by saying, "I go to mass because my parents go." But one day I heard his father talking to my father: "Betty and I go to mass for the kids," *(Several coughs are heard.)* I know when I was young, I liked going to church because right after mass my father would take us to the bakery. And all four of us — my two sisters and my brother and myself — would pick out what we'd like. I'd almost always get jelly doughnuts and I'd never wait to get home before having one … *(Another cough.)* But

jelly doughnuts aren't a very good reason for going to mass are they? *(Many coughs.)* What are your reasons … *(Two loud coughs. Mark erupts.)* I wonder if the coughing lot of you know, or *try* to know why you pull yourselves out of bed every Sunday morning and come here!? *(Silence.)* Do you need to come to mass? Do you need the church? Ideally, the purpose of the church is to become obsolete. But until it is, we need the habit of coming together and collectively recognizing that there is another world. There is a world that coexists and gives order to this world. Individually we come to mass with our own personal chaos and together we look to be ordered. We must come with our hearts open for that. *(Cell phone rings.)* But you come with your Gap shirts and your cell phones and your blue hair. Those things are your shackles — they are accessories you have *made* essential. *You* are essential. *(Rapid cross-fade from pulpit to office.)*

Scene 5

The office. That afternoon.

Tim, standing above the desk, is on the phone.

TIM. Yes — well, he's very young and high-spirited — like a thoroughbred at the starting gate … I know you come to mass because of me, Helen, but he has to start somewhere. I mean if he were going to be a dentist, there would have to be that first set of molars … I *(House phone buzzes.)* Listen — I have to run, Helen. Oh — and thanks again for the "bubbly" and will you thank Jim for me. Yes — don't worry — I'll be speaking to him very soon. You bet. Thanks for calling, Helen. *(Presses intercom button.)* Yes, Margaret … *(Rises.)* Oh, he is. Send him in. *(Tim goes to his wine cabinet, opens it and takes out a glass. He takes a wine bottle from the cabinet and starts to pour himself a drink as Mark enters dressed in a black clergy suit.)* Well, Mark — the parish poll is in and eighty percent of those interviewed, after having seen the spirit move you, feel that you and the spirit should move each other to that rustic bakery in the Trappist Monastery in the mountains. But take heart. You might be able to persuade the Trappists to expand the bakery — that way you can have jelly doughnuts *every* day.

MARK. Why did you invite the faculty?

TIM. I did not invite the faculty. They came to see Sister Rosalie and her Maryknoll Marionettes. And they were very surprised and thrilled to hear that the purpose of the church is to become obsolete.

MARK. The faculty doesn't matter. You said that the people decide.

TIM. They do.

MARK. Well — they stopped coughing.

TIM. They also stopped breathing. *(Phone buzzes. Tim answers.)* Yes, Margaret ... Tell him I'm out ... Margaret ... this is no time for scruples. I can't deal with Mr. Hartigan now ... What? ... All right, Margaret ... All right, all right, then let me get to him before he gets angry for being kept waiting. *(Presses phone button. He rises.)* Hello, Mr. Hartigan ... Oh you were ... Yes — He's a deacon. Yes — well, he's very young and high-spirited — like a thoroughbred at the starting gate ... I know the church is not a racetrack, Mr. Hartigan ... I'm sorry he made you uncomfortable ... I know you worked hard for everything you owned, but I don't think he was denying that ... I agree there's no need for you to feel shackled ... *(Tim turns and stares at Mark.)* Pardon me? ... Yes — I got the bottle of sparkling Burgundy you and Mrs. Hartigan sent me. Thank you and thank her for me, will you? ... No — not at all — I'm glad you called. It's always good to know the pulse of the parish ... Goodbye Mr. Hartigan. *(He hangs up.)*

MARK. *(Pause. Goes to him.)* Why do you let them do that to you?

TIM. Mark, when I first came to this parish, the people didn't want me. The priest I replaced was well loved and nobody was happy about his transfer. I was compared to him — the men ignored me — the women were painfully polite to me. Rich men in their sick beds chastised me for not coming to visit them sooner. I would come home to my room after my daily rounds and want to burst into tears. I'd get to bed at eleven o'clock and maybe fall asleep by four A.M. I broke out in a rash all over my body except my face and my hands. And whatever kept that rash off my face and my hands got me through. I have now achieved a level of beloved in his parish — a level I have basked in for the last ten years and for which I have never had to fight as hard as I had to this afternoon. Now will you mind telling me what happened to you in that pulpit?

MARK. I gave my alternate sermon.

TIM. You lost control.

MARK. All right — I lost control and I'm glad I did.

TIM. A priest should inspire control.

MARK. This morning I felt like a priest for the first time.

TIM. I don't want to hear about the "spirit moving you."

MARK. I can't explain it any other way. Why does it have to be explained?

TIM. Because nobody's buying that you're a thoroughbred at the starting gate.

MARK. Then don't try to sell them that. It was a mystery to me, let it be a mystery to them. Not everything can be explained, for God's sake. The core of the church is extra-scientific and unexplainable.

TIM. Mark — my congregation is not some sort of primitive tribe who'll watch in awe as their priest becomes possessed by some preternatural force. You can't go on a rampage like that and expect to be understood. I've never had so many phone calls — never. And the collection went down thirty percent. It's no accident that the collection comes after the sermon. It's like the Nielson rating.

MARK. Father — if I'm making things difficult for you here, I'll speak to Monsignor Burke and ask him to let you off the hook, and I'll go back to the seminary. (Silence.)

TIM. Let's move on to Lesson II — Consolations. (Tim opens folder on Mark.) From what I can see here and from what the faculty tell me, you're very active in terms of special projects — the retarded, prisoners, the elderly — but they also say that you have difficulty communicating empathy to an average person going through a life crisis. Do you feel empathy?

MARK. Yes — I just don't know what to say. Everything I think of saying sounds so stupid.

26

TIM. But that's just the idea. Consolations *should* sound stupid so that the person in grief will realize how inconsolable their grief is. Inconsolable grief puts a person in a very exalted position. This feeling of being exalted gets most people through most tragedies. So your responsibility as a priest is to bring common grief to the heights of the inconsolable by saying something inane. Let's give it a try. Hit me with a tragedy.

MARK. What kind?

TIM. A tragedy ... Someone from the parish pulls you aside after mass and says ...

MARK. Uh. My mother passed away last night, Father.

TIM. Now — presuming you knew the deceased and she was over eighty, obviously you'd say, "Well, she had a good life." On the other hand if she'd been ill, you'd say, "It was a merciful release."

MARK. Even I could think of something better that that.

TIM. You're not supposed to. Keep it simple and stupid. This is one the few areas where stupid is smart. Make up another tragedy. *(Mark thinks.)* Hurry. Hurry — just pick one out of pool of human experience and lay it on me.

MARK. *(Out front.)* My baby died in his crib last night.

TIM. That's awful.

MARK. Is that what you'd say?

TIM. What made you think of something like that?

MARK. You said a tragedy.

TIM. You really get into it.

MARK. You told me ...

TIM. All right, all right, all right. If the mother was young, you could say, "You can have another."

MARK. Like an hors d'oeuvre.

TIM. Or you could say he, or she, went straight to heaven.

MARK. I'd rather not say anything.

TIM. But you have to say something.

MARK. Why? Why do I have to *say* something? Can't I just listen?

TIM. No. Now I'll give you one. My father beats me.

MARK. Now I'm supposed to say something inane?

TIM. Right.

MARK. Okay — let me think ... Your father beats you ...

TIM. Right.

27

MARK. *(Faces Tim.)* You don't have any scars; you'd never know it.

TIM. I go to school with black eyes.

MARK. Catholic School?

TIM. What difference would that make?

MARK. Well — they're always fighting in Catholic schools so they all have black eyes. You must fit right in.

TIM. My father left us. We don't know whether he's dead or alive.

MARK. Well — that's okay. Who needs a sadist like that for a father anyway? How am I doing?

TIM. My mother remarried. I hate her new husband.

MARK. Why?

TIM. The church says she can't remarry until it's certain her first husband is dead.

MARK. That's no reason to hate him.

TIM. I cry myself to sleep because I'm sure she's going to hell.

MARK. Do you believe there can be such a thing as hell?

TIM. After a while — I just wouldn't talk to her.

MARK. You talk to her now — don't you?

TIM. She died. We hadn't exchanged a word in two years. *(Silence.)*

MARK. Go on. I'm listening.

TIM. I went into the preparatory seminary when I was thirteen. I believed everything I was taught. Followed all the rules — to the letter. I wanted everyone to be perfect. Especially my mother. When I thought she wasn't, I cut her off. She'd write — she'd call — I never answered. Once she called, and I came so close — I had the phone in my hand. But I hung up. Three weeks later, she was dead. You ask me if I believe there's such a thing as hell. There are hints of it, here, on this earth. *(Mark touches Tim. Tim backs away.)* … That's enough on consolations. Lets move on to Lesson III — Converts. *(The phone buzzes. Tim answers.)* Yes, Margaret … Oh, no … How does he sound? … Oh for … Okay — thank you, Margaret. *(Presses the hold button.)* Mark — could you excuse me for a minute. This is private.

MARK. Should I leave for the day?

TIM. No — just go into the kitchen. Margaret's doing some work there and she'd love the company. I won't be long. *(Mark exits. Tim presses button.)* Hello, Tom. Glad you called. I was just thinking about you. Listen — we never did get a chance to look at those pictures from Barcelona ... could you get ahold of your sister ... Saturday sounds great ... *(Records the date in his appointment book.)* All right — see you then, Tom ... Pardon me? Yes, Mark Dolson did give a sermon. I would have invited you but ... Yes — I think he did say something about the purpose of the church is to become obsolete, but I'm sure he meant it as a joke ... No — nobody laughed ... Tom — I'm sure all of our jobs are safe for at least another five hundred years ... It only "sounded" radical ... Tom — the fact is Mark didn't say anything he didn't have a right to say. Even the faculty said that ... Yes — I'll send him over to you, but you don't have to talk to him about the sermon. I've already showed him what he did wrong ... It's not? ... What do you want to see him about ... I see. But he's always alone. I think he just defended them because he felt they had a right to change. I really don't think it was anything more than that ... yes — I know you like to be sure ... Yes — I'll send him over to you. See you Saturday, Tom. *(He hangs up, rises, calls offstage.)* Mark — can you come in here, please.

MARK. *(From offstage.)* I'm helping Margaret with the dishes.

TIM. Never mind about the dishes. Come in here now.

MARK. *(As he enters, sleeves rolled up, carrying a dish towel.)* I just have few more pot ...

TIM. Monsignor Burke wants to see you right after you finish here.

MARK. He's upset about the sermon.

TIM. He says it's not about the sermon.

MARK. It's not?

TIM. Monsignor Burke has appointments with several seminarians and now — you.

MARK. Why?

TIM. Some dress funny — others hang out together too much —

MARK. What did I do?

TIM. He says you were too vehement in your defense of Frank Kearney and Alfred Virasi. And he wants to talk to you about a possible connection.

MARK. He's nuts.

TIM. That's just the kind of intelligent approach he's hoping you'll resort to.

MARK. Do I have to put up with this? Can't I see the bishop?

TIM. The bishop? The bishop is so paranoid about this Frank and Alfred Business, he wishes all the altar boys were girls. The bishop will let Burke do what he wants.

MARK. What do you think he's going to ask me?

TIM. It's hard to say. These interviews change according to the person he's inter ... Let's do it.

MARK. What?

TIM. The interview. I'll play Monsignor Burke and you play you.

MARK. I shouldn't have to go through this — at all.

TIM. Mark — relax. You don't have to be afraid of anything, do you? Come on — just go out and come in like you're coming for the interview.

MARK. I don't want to play a psycho game.

TIM. Mark — you have to go through this with as much grace and tact as you can. You can't afford a repeat of your last encounter with him. *(Mark doesn't move. Tim goes to him.)* Come on — stop wasting time. I have to get ready for my five-twenty. Now go out and come in.

MARK. All right. *(Mark goes off and re-enters as if coming in for his interview with Monsignor Burke.)*

TIM. *(As Burke.)* Good day, Dolson.

MARK. *(Laughing at the apparent accuracy of the impersonation.)* Hello, Monsignor Burke.

TIM. *(As Burke.)* You're late.

MARK. I am? Well — sorry — I've been fasting all week and meditating every night so time and space are ...

TIM. That's very interesting, Dolson. Tell me, have you considered a career in a contemplative order?

MARK. Funny you should say that. Father Farley suggested that very thing to me just today.

TIM. *(As Burke.)* Well — He manages to come up with a few good ideas every ... *(As himself.)* Leave me out of this. *(As Burke.)* Now — I'd like to ask you a few questions. My first question has to do with Frank Kearney and Alfred Virasi.

MARK. No, he wouldn't get into that right away.

TIM. *(As himself.)* He's a busy man.

MARK. If he's so busy, let him skip my interview.

TIM. *(As himself.)* All right — have it your way. *(As Burke.)* How's your family?

MARK. Fine — thank you.

TIM. *(As Burke.)* There's one thing I've always been curious about, Dolson, in regards to your family life. Why did you leave home at sixteen?

MARK. I wanted to be on my own.

TIM. But so young. Was there something at home pushing you out?

MARK. I don't think I realized it at the time, but there was a silence in my house that ... crushed me. There were choruses going on inside of me, and at dinner we all chewed and clanked — and there were times I thought the fork would melt right in my hand.

TIM. So you left?

MARK. Yes.

TIM. And they let you go?

MARK. I think they were relieved.

TIM. Where did you go?

MARK. *(Pause.)* What were you asking about Frank and Alfred?

TIM. *(As Burke.)* Well ... I have been wondering why you reacted so strongly to my suggestion that they take off a year from their studies.

MARK. It was not a suggestion — it was a demand. They did not take a year off — You kicked them out.

TIM. All right — if you want to be direct. *(As Burke.)* Do you think priests should be allowed to sleep together?

MARK. They weren't priests — They weren't even deacons. A vow of celibacy was far off for them.

TIM. *(As Burke.)* Do you think such practices are easily dispensed with?

MARK. Practices? Could you be more specific, Monsignor?

TIM. *(As Burke.)* Just answer my question. *(As himself.)* Just answer his question.

MARK. Is your question something along the lines of, "How you gonna keep 'em down on the farm after they've seen Paree?"

TIM. *(As Burke.)* Stop your verbal acrobatics and give a response to whatever you interpret my question to be.

MARK. Yes — I think Frank and Alfred would have stayed down on the farm after they had seen Paree.

TIM. *(As Burke.)* Let me ask my next question in your native tongue. Have *you* ever seen Paree? *(Silence.)* And if you have seen Paree — were they Parisiettes or ... Parisians?

MARK. *(Long pause.)* Both.

TIM. *(As himself.)* Really?

MARK. That's it — no more. You were shocked.

TIM. I was playing Monsignor Burke. Both?

MARK. Yes — women and men — two sexes. Monsignor — before I came to the seminary, I enrolled myself in a three-year orgy that laid waste to every fiber of my character. Does that sound apologetic enough? How about this? Monsignor Burke — please understand — I explored the world by indulging my sexual ambivalence. I searched, with my body, and I discovered that I could never reconcile my inner emotional world that way. Others have — but my unique, personal and human condition called for another way. So I invite celibacy. I will be happy to stay down on the farm because it's there I will be calm enough to help others. And the only real joy in this world is helping other people. I feel determined and perfectly prepared to become a priest. What would he say to that?

TIM. *(As Burke.)* Both?

MARK. Will you stop?

TIM. I'm sorry — It's just that I've never seen you in this light before.

MARK. What light?

TIM. Red light.

MARK. And you've *never* been in "red light"?

TIM. By the time my father left and my mother died, I was so confused I didn't want to be near man, woman or piano leg. Celibacy came naturally to me. Mark — if Monsignor Burke asks you, say — "Yes — I did make love with Parisiettes."

MARK. That's a half-truth.

TIM. Don't start throwing principles around now, Mark. This is too serious for principles. In the larger scheme of things, Monsignor Burke is not that important.

MARK. But the truth is. I won't become a priest on a lie.

TIM. Better that than not at all.

MARK. I can't believe you're saying this. I won't listen. *(Mark starts to go.)*

TIM. All right — don't listen to me. Go over there and do your martyr number. Just leave your forwarding address behind. *(Mark goes to Tim.)*

MARK. He can't get rid of me.

TIM. He *can* get rid of you. Mark — once you become a priest you can fight him all you like. You'll probably end up hearing confessions in the cornfields of Iowa, but at least give yourself a chance. Make sure you do become a priest. Try it my way. Be diplomatic. Avoid answering questions directly. You can steer the questions. Phrase your answers certain ways ...

MARK. You mean lie.

TIM. Even Christ said to his apostles, "Be as innocent as doves and as cunning as serpents." Christ said that.

MARK. Does cunning mean lying?

TIM. If you can afford not to be a priest — tell the truth. If you want to be a priest — lie. *(Silence.)* Mark — I want you to become a priest. I asked for you.

MARK. You asked for me? You said ...

TIM. I know. I told you Monsignor Burke made me do this, that he forced this special assignment on me. He didn't. I asked him to let me help you.

MARK. Why?

TIM. Because you're a lunatic. And the church needs lunatics — you're one of those priceless lunatics that come along every so often and makes the church alive. The only problem with lunatics is they don't know how to survive. I do. *(Pause. Holds out his keys.)* Here — take my car. *(Mark hesitates, then takes the keys as the lights fade to black.)*

End of Act One

33

ACT TWO

Scene 1

Lights come up on the office. Tim is waiting. He pours himself a drink. House phone buzzes. He answers.

TIM. Yes, Margaret ... Yes — Yes — send him in. *(Mark enters, wearing his black clerical suit.)* Well? *(Mark puts the car keys on the desk.)* What happened?
MARK. *(After silence, Mark jumps into the air.)* It was great!
TIM. What happened?
MARK. What a feeling!
TIM. What did you say?
MARK. I just sat there with my arm flung over the back of the chair.
TIM. You shouldn't have done that. You might have antagonized him.
MARK. I was just being confident.
TIM. Nothing is more antagonistic than confidence. You should have hugged yourself and rocked back and forth. Now tell me what happened?
MARK. Everything's fine.
TIM. He didn't ask you.
MARK. He did.
TIM. Oh — You had to lie. I'm sorry, Mark, but you see these things ...
MARK. I didn't lie.
TIM. You didn't lie?
MARK. I told him the truth.
TIM. You told him the truth?
MARK. I had to.

34

TIM. What do you mean, you "had to"?

MARK. It's all right.

TIM. Did he ask about me?

MARK. Yes — he wanted to know if you knew, and I told him you did, but you thought it was just fine because you've given up Margaret for Mr. Hartigan.

TIM. Mark —

MARK. Relax — We stayed clear of you.

TIM. I wish you had listened to me.

MARK. Why? Everything's fine. You were wrong about him. And you were wrong about lying.

TIM. I was wrong? All right — fine. Just tell me — when you said "both" what did he say?

MARK. He said, "Thank you for being so honest — Good day."

TIM. That's all he said?

MARK. Yes. Isn't that great?

TIM. "Thank you for being so honest — Good day."

MARK. Right. You see?

TIM. "Thank you for being so honest. Good day."

MARK. Why are you repeating what he said? *(Silence.)* Now don't start reading into this. Why would he thank me for being honest if he didn't ... No — I'm not going to dissect it ... You interpret it your way and I'll ... I'll interpret it mine ... *(Mark repeats.)* "Thank you for being so honest — Good day." I'm in trouble. God — I am so deaf. He sent me to your dialogue sermon. That seemed very innocent. He expelled Frank and Alfred and called it "Taking a leave of absence." And now — "Thank you for being so honest — Good day." Which means he's going to get rid of me — isn't he? Isn't he? *(Silence.)* Will you help me?

TIM. I can't.

MARK. Why not?

TIM. You told the truth. If I defended you to him, the same thing that's happening to you would happen to me.

MARK. But it's wrong. Burke gets away with this crap because only one or two people will say anything. The whole parish should get after him. He can't implicate the entire parish.

TIM. True — but ...

MAR. You said the people in your parish can influence him.

TIM. They can …

MARK. And you have influence over them.

TIM. I do, but …

MARK. Can't you talk to them about this?

TIM. Well … not really.

MARK. Why not?

TIM. Well — because he hasn't done anything yet. He's just asked you a few questions.

MARK. But we both know he will do something and by the time he does it will be too late to get their help. Will you please talk to them?

TIM. Mark — The fact of the matter is, after that sermon you gave, if I went to the people in my parish and told them Burke was going to dump you, they would send him "thank you" cards.

MARK. Why should it matter what they think of me? There's an issue here.

TIM. You *are* the issue. *(Pause.)* What I might be willing to do is to let you give another sermon.

MARK. What would that do?

TIM. The only way you would stand a chance of getting help from the people in my parish is by redeeming yourself with them.

MARK. Burke won't let you do that.

TIM. He hasn't told me you can't give any more sermons yet and if I avoid him for the next week, which is an appealing prospect, I could get away with it.

MARK. Isn't there another way?

TIM. Take the help on my terms, or not at all.

MARK. *(Pause.)* I don't know what to say to them.

TIM. We'll call this your redemption sermon. Forget about Norman Rockwell — We have to go deeper this time. Tell them what made you decide become a priest. Tell them why you want to help them. I'll pass out reaction sheets so we can see how effective you're being.

MARK. "Reaction sheets?"

TIM. It'll save wear and tear on the phone. Give them something concrete — like my street corner.

MARK. Your what?

TIM. My street corner … never mind. Just think of specifics —

like a teacher, a best friend — no, we better stay away from best friends for now — a favorite saint, a confirmation name, a pet ...

MARK. I had a tank of tropical fish. Someone turned up the tank heater and they all boiled.

TIM. That's very interesting — and someday you and I will sit down and relive the whole experience, but right now I don't think boiled fish will melt their hearts. Maybe if you say *Going My Way* or if a priest saved your little brother's life — something like that — but they won't relate to guppies.

MARK. What *can* they relate to? Bingo? A car sweepstake? The Lottery?

TIM. Mark — relax. *(Pause.)* You know — maybe we have this problem in reverse. Maybe it's not so much getting the people to like you as it is getting you to ... What do you feel for those people you want help from?

MARK. What do you feel for them?

TIM. I'm asking you.

MARK. I can't just *say* what I feel for them.

TIM. Yes you can.

MARK. I ... I love them.

TIM. How do you love them? Intellectually?

MARK. No.

TIM. You really care for them?

MARK. Yes ... yes ... I ...

TIM. Then why do you offend them?

MARK. I don't mean to.

TIM. Why do you?

MARK. I know what they could be.

TIM. But Mark — what about what they are? What are they to you?

MARK. *(Pause.)* They're my family. They get to me. But I don't know how to get to them. Show me. *(Silence.)*

TIM. St. Francis got completely undressed in the middle of his town square — He gave all his clothes back to his father, and then he was ready to begin. Do the same — be naked — and then talk to the people. Talk to them — as if they were one person — talk to them as if ... they were me.

MARK. I had a tank of tropical fish. *(The lights on the pulpit get brighter as the lights in the office start to dim.)* Someone turned up the tank heater and they all boiled. *(Mark moves slowly to the pulpit as he speaks.)*

Scene 2

Mark is in the pulpit.

MARK. I woke up on a Friday morning and I went to feed them — and there they were — all of my beautiful fish floating on the top. Most of them split in two. Others with their eyes hanging out. It looked like violence, but it was such a quiet night. And I remember wishing that I had the kind of ears that could hear fish screams because they looked as if they had suffered and I wanted so badly to save them. That Sunday in church, I heard that Christ told his apostles to be fishers of men. From then on, I looked at all the people in the church as fish. I was young so I saw them as beautiful tropical fish, and so I knew they were all quiet screamers. Church was so quiet. And I thought everyone was boiling. And I wanted the kind of ears that could hear what they were screaming about, because I wanted to save them. *(Pause.)* A few years later, the people in the church lost the stained-glass look of tropical fish, and they became catfish to me — over-dressed scavengers. So I drowned out whatever I might be able to hear. I made my world — my tank — so hot that I almost split. So now I'm back — listening — listening for the screams of angels. *(The lights dim.)*

Scene 3

Lights come up on the office on a Monday morning. Tim has been drinking. Tim has a bottle in his right hand, a glass in his left. Mark enters watching Tim as he pours wine into his glass.

TIM. *(Seeing Mark.)* Well, Mark — we have loads of reactions.

MARK. Isn't it a little early to be drinking?

TIM. It's just wine. Making wine was Christ's first miracle. He knew what he was doing?

MARK. Did you have breakfast?

TIM. Never mind about that ...

MARK. You should at least eat something ...

TIM. You have to hear these reactions ...

MARK. I don't want to.

TIM. They're not bad, Mark. I think we might have a chance. Let me just read a few.

MARK. Only if you put down the wine.

TIM. All right — all right — As if you didn't have enough causes on hand. Now! I'll start with the worst and work up to the best. Are you ready?

MARK. Just read it.

TIM. Now here is the worst. *(Reading)* "We have no choice but to be catfish with garbage like that being thrown at us." That's the worst. Well, it's not *that* bad. I know him — Mr. Jennings — he's a convert — ah, he's a jerk — never mind about him.

MARK. Don't read anymore.

TIM. They get better. "Father — I don't know if we're fish, but we're certainly not boiling. It's freezing in that church. Is there any way to turn up the heat, just a little?" It's not negative. Here's the next one. Oh, now listen to this. "Dear Father Farley — He is a very sweet boy. I had a goldfish once that died from chlorine in the city water so I know just how he feels. I wrote to the city complaining about the amount of chlorine in their water and they told me … " And she goes on and on, but she likes you. Now listen to this one — "Father — He shows unusual sensitivity. It's very exciting to watch such a change. You're doing good work." I wrote that. No — only kidding. Someone in the parish wrote it — honest. And here's the final one — which I hesitate to read to you, but — "Don't take this the wrong way, Father, but Mark Dolson is just great. Can he give sermons every Sunday?" What do you think? *(Gives reaction sheets to Mark.)*

MARK. I don't know. What does it mean?

TIM. It means there's hope. They're starting to like you.

MARK. What do we do next?

TIM. Before we do anything, I'm going to call up Mr. Jennings and tell him what a jerk he is. *(Reaches for the phone.)*

MARK. *(Going to phone and putting his hand on the receiver.)* Father, no!

TIM. "Garbage" — Who does he think he is?

MARK. Will you just sit down.

TIM. Well — he pisses me off.

MARK. It's all right.

TIM. Well — he does. *(Tim reaches for the phone.)*

MARK. *(His hand on the phone.)* Don't. He might fight back.

TIM. You think I'm a coward, don't you? Just because I won't make an appeal for you, you think …

MARK. Let's not get into it right now.

TIM. Well maybe I will. You don't know what I'll do. *(House phone buzzes. Both reach for the phone.)*

MARK. You shouldn't talk to anyone.

TIM. Will you calm down. I'm fine. *(Presses intercom button.)* Yes, Margaret — Oh he does? *(To Mark.)* It's "Boyke." *(Into phone.)* Margaret — I just realized I haven't had any breakfast. Could you do something about that? … Oh. *(To Mark.)* Mark — I've already had my breakfast.

MARK. You can't talk to him.

TIM. Yes, I can talk to him.

MARK. You're going to get in trouble. Give me the phone.

TIM. No. You'll think I'm a coward. Let me talk to him. *(Silence.)* Father … please. *(Tim surrenders the phone.)*

MARK. *(On phone.)* Hello, Monsignor — This is Mark Dolson —

I'm taking Father Farley's calls right now ... Yes — we meet more regularly. And I didn't get a chance during our last meeting to thank you for making this special arrangement. It's been ... Yes, I did give another sermon — I was only hoping to make up for the one I had given earlier ... I'm sorry if the people you spoke with thought it was inane. I was only trying to ... I see. Is that decision final? ... Two weeks ... Monsignor — I think what you're doing is a sin ... Yes, I'll tell Father Farley to call you. *(Mark hangs up.)*

TIM. What happened?

MARK. It's official. He wants me out. *(Pause.)* Damn him! This is not right. He can't make decisions like that. I'm going to fight him. I have one more Sunday left. All I'm asking is that you let me make my own appeal in my own way at your mass.

TIM. You can't make an appeal for yourself. That's like nominating yourself for president.

MARK. Who else will do it?

TIM. It's not necessary. You're getting carried away. *(Tim goes to the phone.)* I'll handle this.

MARK. How?

TIM. I'm going to call up Monsignor Burke.

MARK. No.

TIM. Yes — I'm going to call him right now.

MARK. *(Puts hand on telephone.)* No — you're drunk.

TIM. I am at my best when I'm drunk. I'm not your typical drunk. *(Removes Mark's hands from phone. Tim dials.)* I think more clearly — speak more clearly — my vocabulary is better. This is the best possible time for me to call Burke ... *(Yells into phone.)* Monsignor Burke, please ... Oh, hello, Tom — Mark told me you called ... Now just slow down, Tom — I can do whatever I want in my parish. Don't presume more authority than you ... It was a good sermon. Mark has made incredible strides ... Yes, he told me and I totally disagree with your decision. This whole sexual question is ridiculous. Celibacy is celibacy even if your thing is goats ... goats. He will keep his vows ... What? ... Yes — I'm keeping mine. What are you ... Tom — there are limits ... No — I will not be threatened. Tom ... Tom ... If I decide Mark gives another sermon, then that's what he'll do. If I decide to give a sermon about Mark, then that's what I'll do. You are not going to intimidate me with your Gestapo tactic. And another thing — I had a terrible time in Barcelona. Goodbye, Monsignor. *(He hangs up the phone.)* I'll do it.

MARK. What?

TIM. I'll make an appeal for you.

MARK. You don't mean it. It's the wine …

TIM. I do mean it. It's not the wine. I'm going to cash in my popularity stock for power.

MARK. What do you mean, "cash in?"

TIM. My people will flood Monsignor Burke with letters and phone calls …

MARK. What if they don't? What if it doesn't work? What will happen to you?

TIM. If I make an appeal for you at my mass next Sunday, and it doesn't work, Burke will go to the bishop and make sure I'm in Iowa by Tuesday. But my people won't let me go. They won't let anything happen to me. So I'm not afraid of Burke. I've prayed for that. I prayed not to be afraid. And right here and now — I'm not. I'm not afraid! *(Blackout.)*

Scene 4

The church. Sunday morning.

Tim enters the pulpit.

TIM. There are all forms of persecution. I'm sure if we watch the six o'clock news for a week, we'd be bound to see almost every kind. But what about the ones that occur right here in this parish? The ones we can do something about. For example: Mark Dolson. He is being persecuted and we should respond. *(Pause.)* Now I'm not trying to impose a sense of guilt on all of us. We're trying to get away from that sort of thing in the Church today. But still, Mark is being persecuted. *(Pause.)* Well — perhaps persecuted is

42

too strong a word. Mark has run into some trouble at St. Francis Seminary, and he needs our help. *(Pause.)* Now some of you might say that Mark can take care of himself. And that's true. Others of you might say that Mark asks for trouble. And that is also true. We've all seen how vehement he can be. So you might say Mark *doesn't* need our help. And you're probably right. But it's good to know that if he did need our help — we would be there. Let us pray. *(The lights quickly fade as Tim leaves the pulpit.)*

Scene 5

The office. Lights come up on Mark wearing street clothes. Tim enters. Tim sees Mark is out of uniform. Silence.

MARK. You wanted to see me.

TIM. Yes. Where did you go?

MARK. To the seminary. To pack.

TIM. What will you do?

MARK. I'm not sure.

TIM. *(Pause.)* Maybe there's another diocese you might be able to go to. I'll make some inquiries. *(Goes to the desk, then stops.)* I suppose — whoever we call would want references from Monsignor Burke — wouldn't they? *(Silence.)* I'm sorry if I got your hopes up. But I was wrong. They would let me go. I saw that in their faces. Didn't you see it? *(Pause.)* You have to understand, Mark ... whatever I said I'd do was above and beyond the call of duty.

MARK. I understand.

TIM. No, I don't think you do. Do you know what a town in Iowa is like? It might have a Main Street. If they have a movie theatre, it only shows "chain saw" movies. The people would not understand my humor. They wouldn't talk to me. I have to talk to people.

MARK. Then why don't you?

TIM. I do. *(Silence.)* Well — if I can help you find a job or if you ever need a recommendation for one, let me know. *(Tim goes to his appointment book.)* I have to kick you out now. I have an appointment coming here any minute.

MARK. *(Not moving.)* No, you don't.

TIM. What?

MARK. You don't have an appointment.

TIM. Are you saying I'm lying?

MARK. Yes.

TIM. Why would I lie about a thing like that?

MARK. I don't know why you lie — I can just tell when you do.

TIM. Now look, you better go.

MARK. But it's all right. They're all harmless lies. You only do it to spare other people's feelings, right?

TIM. I liked it better when you weren't talking. You have to go. *(Mark doesn't move. Silence.)* Whether you believe me or not, I have an appointment coming here any minute now.

MARK. An appointment. Really? Which "human condition" is it today? An abortion? A divorce? Or an identity crisis?

TIM. None of your business.

MARK. Why don't you give a break to whoever it is and cancel?

TIM. I know you think you have a right to be angry with me ...

MARK. I'm not angry with you.

TIM. You are ... you think I betrayed you.

MARK. What you did or didn't do for me doesn't make any difference now. I believed you, because I needed to believe you. I set myself up — that's not your fault. But the people who come to you for help deserve more.

TIM. Never mind about the people that come here for my help. They're taken care of.

MARK. You handle them — I've seen it — the way you handled me. You say what everyone wants to hear. Doesn't matter if it's true of if you can back up what you say, as long as you pacify whoever is on the other side of the desk. You'll say anything to get a person in need off your back.

TIM. Mark, get out.

MARK. No. I think I should stay here until your "appointment" comes.

TIM. Would you please leave?

MARK. I should warn whoever it is. *(Mark advances toward Tim.)*

44

People should be warned about you.

TIM. Don't push me.

MARK. They all come here thinking they're being helped — But really, all they're doing is pouring their guts out to a drunk who catalogs their anguish.

TIM. Get out! *(Tim punches Mark in the stomach. A long pause.)* I think I broke my wrist.

MARK. I'm sorry.

TIM. It's broken — I know it.

MARK. It can't be.

TIM. It bent back.

MARK. You don't know how to punch.

TIM. I never had a reason to.

MARK. Maybe it's sprained. Twirl your arm around.

TIM. What?

MARK. Twirl your arm around. Like this. *(He demonstrates a wide circular motion with his arm. Tim tries it while seated and hits his arm on the back of the chair. He then rises and moves away from the chair.)* Twirl your arm around. Like this. *(Repeats movement.)*

TIM. *(Copies Mark.)* What's this supposed to do?

MARK. It's for ... it ... it's supposed to ... I don't know. I don't know what it's supposed to do.

TIM. You don't know?

MARK. No ... *(Mark starts laughing. Tim joins the laughter. Tim's laughter turns to tears.)* Father ... *(Tim sits. Silence.)*

TIM. I tried Mark — I wanted to help you — but I need them.

MARK. I understand. I do. During those three years — whenever someone I loved loved me, I did everything I could to keep it constant. Bit by bit — through trial and error — I learned all the rules — what to say — what to give — what to withhold — so I could keep the love constant. But to go through all that — to worry about who's got the upper hand — who's going to change first — it made the love worthless. I found out that the constant is up to me. Promises are broken; friends will be fickle; love goes its own course, and all of it has to ultimately not matter. And what you believe has to be more important than what your congregation thinks of you.

TIM. Mark. I'm not sure what I believe anymore. *(Church bell*

45

chimes.) The five-twenty mass! *(He rushes to his vestments.)* It's the most attended mass of the day. Standing room only. *(Pause.)* And I have nothing prepared. *(Pause.)* I can't face them. I can't.

MARK. Yes, you can. *(Mark dresses Tim for Mass.)*

TIM. What about you?

MARK. I'll be fine.

TIM. Where will you go?

MARK. For now, I think I should go back to the seminary and finish packing. *(They shake hands. Tim grabs his right hand in pain.)*

TIM. Ow. *(Pause.)* Mark, did you know, when Christ sent his apostles out into the world, he sent them in twos. I think I know why he did that now. *(There is nothing more to say. Mark exits.)*

Scene 6

The 5:20 mass. Tim is in the pulpit.

TIM. This evening we were supposed to conclude our "On the Road to the Priesthood" series. But I have nothing prepared. And that's not like me. I'm always prepared. So much so, that I haven't really talked to you since I've been here. Because — you see — I've lost Christ. I missed him. I just tap danced right past him. When I was on the street corner ... well ... There, you were just people on your way to somewhere, but you stopped, to listen, to me. And there — I knew what I wanted to say to you, but I didn't know how. Now — I know *how* ... but from here — I haven't really been a very good priest to you. From here — I never really cared enough to run the risk of losing you. From here — I can't really see your faces. *(Tim leaves the pulpit to address the people.)* Monsignor Burke has expelled Mark Dolson from St. Francis Seminary and consequently he is barred from the priesthood. Monsignor Burke will tell you that he has expelled Mark because of his past ... because prior to his decision to become a priest, Mark made love with women and with men. But I don't believe that's the real reason. I believe Mark's past is irrelevant. I believe Monsignor Burke has looked for and found a way to get rid of Mark because Mark threatens Monsignor Burke's picture of what the church should be. But this is not only Monsignor Burke's church. This is our church. Fight for it. Tell him you will not accept his decision. We have to show him what Mark has shown me — that you and I and Mark must be allowed to help shape the thing that has shaped us. *(Pause.)* This is the first time I haven't tried to win your love. Only now is love possible. *(Pause.)* Oh, by the way — if you don't see me up here next week, I'll probably be in Iowa. But for now, for as long as I'm here ... Let us ... begin. *(The lights fade to black as music swells.)*

End of Play

PROPERTY LIST

Sheet of paper (TIM)
Bottle of wine and glasses (TIM)
Note pad (TIM)
Tape recorder (TIM)
Notes for sermon (TIM)
Phone (TIM, MARK)
Priedieu (TIM)
Folders containing papers (TIM)
Bottle of sparkling Burgundy (TIM)
Red pencil (TIM)
Appointment book and pen (TIM)
Dish towel (MARK)
Keys (TIM, MARK)
Papers (TIM)
Vestments (TIM)

SOUND EFFECTS

Phone buzzes
Coughs
Cell phone rings
Church bell chimes
Music

NEW PLAYS

★ **MONTHS ON END by Craig Pospisil.** In comic scenes, one for each month of the year, we follow the intertwined worlds of a circle of friends and family whose lives are poised between happiness and heartbreak. "...a triumph...these twelve vignettes all form crucial pieces in the eternal puzzle known as human relationships, an area in which the playwright displays an assured knowledge that spans deep sorrow to unbounded happiness." –*Ann Arbor News*. "...rings with emotional truth, humor...[an] endearing contemplation on love...entertaining and satisfying." –*Oakland Press*. [5M, 5W] ISBN: 0-8222-1892-5

★ **GOOD THING by Jessica Goldberg.** Brings us into the households of John and Nancy Roy, forty-something high-school guidance counselors whose marriage has been increasingly on the rocks and Dean and Mary, recent graduates struggling to make their way in life. "...a blend of gritty social drama, poetic humor and unsubtle existential contemplation..." –*Variety*. [3M, 3W] ISBN: 0-8222-1869-0

★ **THE DEAD EYE BOY by Angus MacLachlan.** Having fallen in love at their Narcotics Anonymous meeting, Billy and Shirley-Diane are striving to overcome the past together. But their relationship is complicated by the presence of Sorin, Shirley-Diane's fourteen-year-old son, a damaged reminder of her dark past. "...a grim, insightful portrait of an unmoored family..." –*NY Times*. "MacLachlan's play isn't for the squeamish, but then, tragic stories delivered at such an unrelenting fever pitch rarely are." –*Variety*. [1M, 1W, 1 boy] ISBN: 0-8222-1844-5

★ **[SIC] by Melissa James Gibson.** In adjacent apartments three young, ambitious neighbors come together to discuss, flirt, argue, share their dreams and plan their futures with unequal degrees of deep hopefulness and abject despair. "A work...concerned with the sound and power of language..." –*NY Times*. "...a wonderfully original take on urban friendship and the comedy of manners—a *Design for Living* for our times..." –*NY Observer*. [3M, 2W] ISBN: 0-8222-1872-0

★ **LOOKING FOR NORMAL by Jane Anderson.** Roy and Irma's twenty-five-year marriage is thrown into turmoil when Roy confesses that he is actually a woman trapped in a man's body, forcing the couple to wrestle with the meaning of their marriage and the delicate dynamics of family. "Jane Anderson's bittersweet transgender domestic comedy-drama ...is thoughtful and touching and full of wit and wisdom. A real audience pleaser." –*Hollywood Reporter*. [5M, 4W] ISBN: 0-8222-1857-7

★ **ENDPAPERS by Thomas McCormack.** The regal Joshua Maynard, the old and ailing head of a mid-sized, family-owned book-publishing house in New York City, must name a successor. One faction in the house backs a smart, "pragmatic" manager, the other faction a smart, "sensitive" editor and both factions fear what the other's man could do to this house— and to them. "If Kaufman and Hart had undertaken a comedy about the publishing business, they might have written *Endpapers*...a breathlessly fast, funny, and thoughtful comedy ...keeps you amused, guessing, and often surprised...profound in its empathy for the paradoxes of human nature." –*NY Magazine*. [7M, 4W] ISBN: 0-8222-1908-5

★ **THE PAVILION by Craig Wright.** By turns poetic and comic, romantic and philosophical, this play asks old lovers to face the consequences of difficult choices made long ago. "The script's greatest strength lies in the genuineness of its feeling." –*Houston Chronicle*. "Wright's perceptive, gently witty writing makes this familiar situation fresh and thoroughly involving." –*Philadelphia Inquirer*. [2M, 1W (flexible casting)] ISBN: 0-8222-1898-4

DRAMATISTS PLAY SERVICE, INC.
440 Park Avenue South, New York, NY 10016 212-683-8960 Fax 212-213-1539
postmaster@dramatists.com www.dramatists.com

NEW PLAYS

★ **BE AGGRESSIVE by Annie Weisman.** Vista Del Sol is paradise, sandy beaches, avocado-lined streets. But for seventeen-year-old cheerleader Laura, everything changes when her mother is killed in a car crash, and she embarks on a journey to the Spirit Institute of the South where she can learn "cheer" with Bible belt intensity. "...filled with lingual gymnastics...stylized rapid-fire dialogue..." –*Variety.* "...a new, exciting, and unique voice in the American theatre..." –*BackStage West.* [1M, 4W, extras] ISBN: 0-8222-1894-1

★ **FOUR by Christopher Shinn.** Four people struggle desperately to connect in this quiet, sophisticated, moving drama. "...smart, broken-hearted...Mr. Shinn has a precocious and forgiving sense of how power shifts in the game of sexual pursuit...He promises to be a playwright to reckon with..." –*NY Times.* "A voice emerges from an American place. It's got humor, sadness and a fresh and touching rhythm that tell of the loneliness and secrets of life...[a] poetic, haunting play." –*NY Post.* [3M, 1W] ISBN: 0-8222-1850-X

★ **WONDER OF THE WORLD by David Lindsay-Abaire.** A madcap picaresque involving Niagara Falls, a lonely tour-boat captain, a pair of bickering private detectives and a husband's dirty little secret. "Exceedingly whimsical and playfully wicked. Winning and genial. A top-drawer production." –*NY Times.* "Full frontal lunacy is on display. A most assuredly fresh and hilarious tragicomedy of marital discord run amok...absolutely hysterical..." –*Variety.* [3M, 4W (doubling)] ISBN: 0-8222-1863-1

★ **QED by Peter Parnell.** Nobel Prize-winning physicist and all-around genius Richard Feynman holds forth with captivating wit and wisdom in this fascinating biographical play that originally starred Alan Alda. "QED is a seductive mix of science, human affections, moral courage, and comic eccentricity. It reflects on, among other things, death, the absence of God, travel to an unexplored country, the pleasures of drumming, and the need to know and understand." –*NY Magazine.* "Its rhythms correspond to the way that people—even geniuses—approach and avoid highly emotional issues, and it portrays Feynman with affection and awe." –*The New Yorker.* [1M, 1W] ISBN: 0-8222-1924-7

★ **UNWRAP YOUR CANDY by Doug Wright.** Alternately chilling and hilarious, this deliciously macabre collection of four bedtime tales for adults is guaranteed to keep you awake for nights on end. "Engaging and intellectually satisfying...a treat to watch." –*NY Times.* "Fiendishly clever. Mordantly funny and chilling. Doug Wright teases, freezes and zaps us." –*Village Voice.* "Four bite-size plays that bite back." –*Variety.* [flexible casting] ISBN: 0-8222-1871-2

★ **FURTHER THAN THE FURTHEST THING by Zinnie Harris.** On a remote island in the middle of the Atlantic secrets are buried. When the outside world comes calling, the islanders find their world blown apart from the inside as well as beyond. "Harris winningly produces an intimate and poetic, as well as political, family saga." –*Independent (London).* "Harris' enthralling adventure of a play marks a departure from stale, well-furrowed theatrical terrain." –*Evening Standard (London).* [3M, 2W] ISBN: 0-8222-1874-7

★ **THE DESIGNATED MOURNER by Wallace Shawn.** The story of three people living in a country where what sort of books people like to read and how they choose to amuse themselves becomes both firmly personal and unexpectedly entangled with questions of survival. "This is a playwright who does not just tell you what it is like to be arrested at night by goons or to fall morally apart and become an aimless yet weirdly contented ghost yourself. He has the originality to make you feel it." –*Times (London).* "A fascinating play with beautiful passages of writing..." –*Variety.* [2M, 1W] ISBN: 0-8222-1848-8

DRAMATISTS PLAY SERVICE, INC.
440 Park Avenue South, New York, NY 10016 212-683-8960 Fax 212-213-1539
postmaster@dramatists.com www.dramatists.com

NEW PLAYS

★ **SHEL'S SHORTS by Shel Silverstein.** Lauded poet, songwriter and author of children's books, the incomparable Shel Silverstein's short plays are deeply infused with the same wicked sense of humor that made him famous. "…[a] childlike honesty and twisted sense of humor." *—Boston Herald.* "…terse dialogue and an absurdity laced with a tang of dread give [*Shel's Shorts*] more than a trace of Samuel Beckett's comic existentialism." *—Boston Phoenix.* [flexible casting] ISBN: 0-8222-1897-6

★ **AN ADULT EVENING OF SHEL SILVERSTEIN by Shel Silverstein.** Welcome to the darkly comic world of Shel Silverstein, a world where nothing is as it seems and where the most innocent conversation can turn menacing in an instant. These ten imaginative plays vary widely in content, but the style is unmistakable. "…[*An Adult Evening*] shows off Silverstein's virtuosic gift for wordplay…[and] sends the audience out…with a clear appreciation of human nature as perverse and laughable." *—NY Times.* [flexible casting] ISBN: 0-8222-1873-9

★ **WHERE'S MY MONEY? by John Patrick Shanley.** A caustic and sardonic vivisection of the institution of marriage, laced with the author's inimitable razor-sharp wit. "…Shanley's gift for acid-laced one-liners and emotionally tumescent exchanges is certainly potent…" *—Variety.* "…lively, smart, occasionally scary and rich in reverse wisdom." *—NY Times.* [3M, 3W] ISBN: 0-8222-1865-8

★ **A FEW STOUT INDIVIDUALS by John Guare.** A wonderfully screwy comedy-drama that figures Ulysses S. Grant in the throes of writing his memoirs, surrounded by a cast of fantastical characters, including the Emperor and Empress of Japan, the opera star Adelina Patti and Mark Twain. "Guare's smarts, passion and creativity skyrocket to awesome heights…" *—Star Ledger.* "…precisely the kind of good new play that you might call an everyday miracle…every minute of it is fresh and newly alive…" *—Village Voice.* [10M, 3W] ISBN: 0-8222-1907-7

★ **BREATH, BOOM by Kia Corthron.** A look at fourteen years in the life of Prix, a Bronx native, from her ruthless girl-gang leadership at sixteen through her coming to maturity at thirty. "…vivid world, believable and eye-opening, a place worthy of a dramatic visit, where no one would want to live but many have to." *—NY Times.* "…rich with humor, terse vernacular strength and gritty detail…" *—Variety.* [1M, 9W] ISBN: 0-8222-1849-6

★ **THE LATE HENRY MOSS by Sam Shepard.** Two antagonistic brothers, Ray and Earl, are brought together after their father, Henry Moss, is found dead in his seedy New Mexico home in this classic Shepard tale. "…His singular gift has been for building mysteries out of the ordinary ingredients of American family life…" *—NY Times.* "…rich moments …Shepard finds gold." *—LA Times.* [7M, 1W] ISBN: 0-8222-1858-5

★ **THE CARPETBAGGER'S CHILDREN by Horton Foote.** One family's history spanning from the Civil War to WWII is recounted by three sisters in evocative, intertwining monologues. "…bittersweet music—[a] rhapsody of ambivalence…in its modest, garrulous way…theatrically daring." *—The New Yorker.* [3W] ISBN: 0-8222-1843-7

★ **THE NINA VARIATIONS by Steven Dietz.** In this funny, fierce and heartbreaking homage to *The Seagull*, Dietz puts Chekhov's star-crossed lovers in a room and doesn't let them out. "A perfect little jewel of a play…" *—Shepherdstown Chronicle.* "…a delightful revelation of a writer at play; and also an odd, haunting, moving theater piece of lingering beauty." *—Eastside Journal (Seattle).* [1M, 1W (flexible casting)] ISBN: 0-8222-1891-7

DRAMATISTS PLAY SERVICE, INC.
440 Park Avenue South, New York, NY 10016 212-683-8960 Fax 212-213-1539
postmaster@dramatists.com www.dramatists.com